Lean In
The Bible

by
Jay Poole

Cover illustrations by: Ryan Hughes

Copyright © Jay Poole 2020

All rights reserved. No part of this publication may be reproduced, stored in a retrieval system, or transmitted in any form or by any means, mechanical, photocopying, recording or otherwise, without prior permission in writing of the author.

ISBN: 978-0-578-65497-3 (paperback)

TABLE OF CONTENTS

About Jay v
Introduction ix

The Beginning 1
Noah and the Ark 6
Bricks Without Straw 15
David and Goliath 24
Solomon's Temple 30
Cleaning the Temple 35
Reaching the Masses 41
Staying Focused 52
Conclusion 59

Benediction 67
Acknowledgement 69
References 71

ABOUT JAY

Jay and his family reside in Northeast Tennessee. He holds a Masters of Business Administration from Liberty University, a Masters of Education from Milligan University and a Bachelors of Business Administration from East Tennessee State University. He is an American Society for Quality Certified Six Sigma Black Belt (CSSBB), and a Society for Human Resources Management Certified Professional (SHRM-CP). He enjoys spending time with his family, reading and researching ideas to continue learning and growing.

This book is dedicated to Elizabeth, John, Ella and Jackson. Always pursue your dreams. Remember, faith can move mountains. There will be times when you cannot see the end and faith is all you have to go on. Be patient and never forget that turning faith into action can bring about big things.

INTRODUCTION

Proverbs 16:9 NIV
"In their hearts humans plan their course,
But the Lord establishes their steps."

My life started in Atlanta, Ga. As a child the church I attended was Peachtree Presbyterian Church. As I get older, memories of the things I did and people I knew have faded; however, a few things still stand out. I remember the kindness of church staff and our interactions. People who had names like Big Ed and Johnny still remain in the back of my mind. I remember these guys always had smiles on their faces no matter how wet their shirts were from working hard at the church. As a young child, when I had free time, I would be all over the church campus exploring and finding new adventures. On Sundays, I would sit in the service while the minister, Rev. Dr. W. Frank Harrington, would lead the sermon lesson. While I knew him as Frank, out of respect he will be referred to as Dr. Harrington. At the conclusion of his services, Dr. Harrington would say,

"Behold, I stand at the door and knock. If anyone hears My voice and opens the door, I will come in to him and dine with him, and he with Me."

The service would then conclude and I would leave.

At the time and at my age, I thought that was pretty cool that Dr. Harrington would invite anyone in the congregation to eat with him. It wasn't until I had a life changing event that I decided to read the New Testament of the Bible. That was when I discovered the Bible verse Dr. Harrington was referencing.

The verse Dr. Harrington was quoting was Revelation 3:20. At my point of discovery I believe I figured out why he was quoting that verse. I believe this verse was being quoted because he wanted the congregation to know God is waiting on us to make the decision to open our hearts and dedicate time to spend with Him. The more I reflect on this verse and how it relates to my life, the more I realize how little I know about what God is doing for me and what he wants me to do with my talents. A number of years have passed and I have continued to recover from my life changing event. During my time of recovery, I can honestly say, while I passively attended church, I was not growing as I felt I should have been when it came to learning more about God and what He wanted me to do with my gifts. After getting married and growing a family, I am only beginning to scratch the surface of who God is and how He has intervened in my life.

A few years ago, to learn more about God I made a commitment to read the Bible. I purchased the twelve-month chronological Bible, which I finished reading in fifteen months. Yes, I said fifteen months. I wish I could say the extra time was due to me spending more time studying chapters and verses. Unfortunately, the additional time was due to me missing days and getting behind. While being behind in accomplishing what was started, I had made a commitment to complete it and even though it was a little delayed, I finished reading it.

I started to see a personal connection shortly after I began reading the Bible. This connection included what I have experienced during my career. The following chapters are biblical events that stood out as process improvement events. Process improvement is a term that focuses on identifying efficiencies, developing methods to address and implementing change to better a process or area. These efficiencies could be equipment related or ways one conducts work. Each Biblical event contains its own dynamic. It is with this understanding that there are many more examples in the Bible of illustrating pivotal events. With that being said, I wanted to focus on these representative scenarios. Further, it is important to note, the Bible does not take time to prove to us that these men were perfect. On the other hand, the Bible tells about how these individuals had flaws and problems they had to work through to be faithful to God in addition to completing the task God had laid before them.

Finally, an understanding that the solution to these biblical events discussed in this book may be investigated and addressed differently. The method I chose is the one that spoke to me. Later in this book there is a chapter about King Solomon. At the time of becoming king, King Solomon asked God for wisdom. I pray that something speaks to you, a desirous thirst develops and moves you toward more knowledge of who God is.

THE BEGINNING

John 1:1 NIV
In the beginning was the Word, and the Word
was with God, and the Word was God.

Have you ever been asked; if you could create the universe, what is the first step you would take? My answer would be to begin with developing a good plan. Throughout history there are good and bad examples of how projects were planned and started. The goal of this chapter is to identify what goes into developing a sound strategy in completing projects.

An example of a project turning bad was the Tacoma Narrows Bridge project, opening in 1940. The bridge was built to provide an avenue for travelers to traverse the Puget Sound from Tacoma, Washington to the Kitsap Peninsula. It was a suspension bridge spanning just over a mile at 5,939 feet. Starting in 1938, it took two years to build the bridge. While being built, lesser quality bridge girders were used to keep costs down. A result of using lesser quality products was, the bridge swayed. Due to the bridge swaying, it was named "Galloping Gertie." Unfortunately, after four months of being open, when winds were high the bridge finally collapsed.[1] As with any project, up front planning is vital to being successful. It is important to ensure the right material is being used. Let's look at the first project ever recorded, God bringing everything into existence, the Creation.

In the beginning there was God. When God brought everything into existence and set all things on earth, He did not just complete the task in one action. He took seven days to complete His vision. Starting with creating the universe. He began with the broad, high level tasks and then, over the next seven days became more specific in his actions until the last day, where he looked at everything he had created and saw that it was good and then He rested. The first three days were focused on creating and maintaining a sustainable environment for animals and humans to live. Once these foundational tasks were complete, He then spent time putting the more detailed items in place. For instance, God placed animals on the earth so humans could have food. Next when the plan was coming to fruition, He placed a man and a woman on earth.[2]

A condensed overview of what He completed:

- Created light
- Separated waters from sky
- Dry ground (vegetation)
- Day and night
- Animals for both water and sky
- Land animals and humans
- REST

How do we plan and prepare to build a foundation for the project we have before us? Depending on the magnitude of the project, the level of detail one chooses to use is important.

When making plans for a project, caution has to be taken to ensure the correct level of detail. There could be a tendency to focus on high level tasks and not take time to dig in to insignificant details. When this happens, there will most likely be problems throughout the project due to failure attributed to poor planning. Some examples of this will include longer build times due to the need to rework strategies or even refabricate equipment. To aid in preventing this from happening, a reasonable timeline should be developed, refined and implemented. Other planning strategies to use are to develop project stages or milestones. Utilizing step-by-step project plan and breaking the project up into performance stages will help eat the proverbial elephant, one bite at a time.[3]

When starting to build a house, what are some items and tasks a project manager needs? Beginning with a sound set of blueprints with related drawings, he will ensure the house sits on a firm foundation. I am over simplifying this example. Basically, the land is staked out to designate key site landmarks. The land is improved to allow the foundation footers to be properly spaced and placed. Through ensuring a sound footing, the house can stand the test of time.

Matthew 7:26-27 NIV:

> "But everyone who hears these words of mine and does not put them into practice is like a foolish man who built his house on sand. The rain came down, the streams rose, and the winds blew and beat against that house, and it fell with a great crash."[4]

Depending on the project, sometimes there is a desire to go straight to the end, not wanting to spend the amount of time to properly complete items identified within the details. Usually when the decision to do this is made, some very important details are missed that make a big difference in how the end result turns out. When God laid out his plan, it is apparent He had taken time to lay the pieces step-by-step in proper order so that when He completed a part of His work, the related other parts would fall in the correct line at the correct time.

During creation there were six days of work and one of rest. Looking at how these days related, God created the realm one day. He then populated it with the objects or beings another day. On the first day He said "Let there be light" and then on the fourth day He separated light from day and night. On the second day, He created the sea and sky, and on the fifth day, he placed animals in the sea and in the sky. Then on the third day, God created land and on the sixth day God populated it with animals. He then looked over what had been completed during the previous six days and said, "It is good."[5]

The below table further clarifies how days were related.[5]

Day One – Light and Dark	Day Four - Separated Light from Day and Night
Day Two – Sea and Sky	Day Five – Placed creatures in the sea and sky
Day Three – Fertile earth	Day Six – populated the land with creatures

The amount of planning and thought God put in is evident in the coordination of each part of creation. Reflecting on all God did to complete creation, for God to say "It is good" instead of "It is finished" infers a meaning that he knew his project wasn't complete. God would have to remain involved for His plan to be accomplished. On a side note, "It is finished" is what Jesus said on the cross. While the entire Bible contains a lot of information one should explore and study, the following chapters comprise stories and analyses pertaining to how God set ordinary people up to lead and accomplish great things.

Chapter Reflection:

1. What strategies do you take when beginning to organize a project/activity?
2. At times, after completing a tough project/activity it is tempting to say we are finished; let's take a break and move on to the next one. While there are many projects that fall into this completion category, what defenses can we put in place to ensure what has been done is maintained?
3. Discuss what you think God meant when he said "It is good"? Do you think God knew he would have to remain involved in this "Project"?

NOAH AND THE ARK

Hebrews 11:7 NIV
By his faith Noah, when warned about things not yet seen, through holy fear built an Ark to save his family.

There is very little said about who Noah was before the flood. When he was born, his father, Lamech, named him Noah, saying, "Out of the ground that the Lord has cursed, this one shall bring us relief from our work and from the painful toil of our hands." The Bible continues to explain how Noah was a righteous man, blameless in his generation. Noah also walked with God.[1] While he is mentioned throughout the Bible, what he accomplished with regards to trade is not mentioned. To have the knowledge to complete such a monumental task, it has been inferred that he was skilled at ship building, as well as being a farmer and preacher.[2] In addition to what has previously been mentioned, the Bible says Noah was a "Preacher of righteousness."[3] Additionally, his father Lamech was alive until the year of the flood so he may have assisted in its design and construction. With this knowledge, we are going to look specifically at the task that was placed before Noah and what was done to ensure he met God's expectations.

So why did Noah need to build the Ark? This story begins with God realizing the people of the earth's thoughts of the heart had turned evil. Seeing how the earth had become filled with wickedness, God's heart was greatly troubled. God decided to wipe them(evil) along with everything else off the earth with a humongous flood. Once complete, He would then rebuild earth with a man who was; righteous, blameless among the people of the time and who walked faithfully with God. God laid out His specific plan, identifying; Ark's design, what material was needed and number of animals Noah would need to re-populate the earth. All this was to be accomplished while ensuring Noah, his family and animals God wanted saved were safe during the flood.[4]

Moving through the preparations of this historical event, God was specific on how Noah was to build the Ark and prepare for the flood. God started by laying out the project specifics:

- Ark
    - Built out of cypress wood.
    - Four hundred fifty feet long, seventy-five feet wide, and forty-five feet high (Based on English translations).
    - Had three levels within the Ark: Lower, Middle and Upper.
    - Made with a roof, leaving below the roof line an opening (transom) one-cubit (approximately 18 inches) high in circumference of the boat.
    - Placed a door in the side of the Ark.
    - Location to store food.

- Ark contents
    - Noah's family.

- Seven pairs of clean animals, male and female.
- One pair of all other animals, male and female.
- Every kind of food to be eaten.

Based off what has been provided, let's consider God is to be the customer and Noah the project lead (manager).

At the beginning of Noah's story, a purpose and a goal for his project was defined:

> **Purpose** – God saw how wicked the human race was and desired for evil to be wiped off the earth. He desired a fresh start through a righteous man and a designated number of animals.
>
> **Goal** – Start fresh and increase in numbers with a morally right human race. Beginning with a righteous man who walked with God and was blameless among the people of his time.

To be successful, the focus on how projects are completed has remained on the customer. Customer satisfaction falls into three categories: Quality, Delivery and Cost. Due to the fact God provided all the necessary resources needed to build the Ark, our focus will be specific to Quality and Delivery.[5]

QUALITY

When God imagined how the Ark was to be built, he was very specific. This point is very important, because the majority of the time a project manager has to formulate the details. He must work with multiple people and groups to fully capture the essence of what needs to be accomplished. Even with the specific plans being handed to him, Noah had to take that information and confirm he did not misinterpret any aspect of the plans. Given resources are not infinite, should he have misinterpreted any part of the design, like a measurement, that would have been costly to the project. To safeguard there were no communication breakdowns, Noah would have needed to confirm where he was within the project. Where there was an item that needed enhanced clarification, he would have to stop and ask for assistance. Finally, he would continue his walk with God throughout this project. By having a relationship with God, he would have been better prepared to make any adjustments as the project developed. Most importantly, God would be up to date with progress and able to provide further direction when needed. Having a strong relationship with the customer and providing frequent plan updates, ensures the quality of the project is compliant at the beginning and end of the project. Throughout the project, outcomes will be to minimize project rework and incurring un-necessary cost.[5]

DELIVERY

It took Noah approximately one hundred years to complete the Ark. While building the Ark, Noah had to focus on protecting the integrity of it. He had to finish and build the Ark in such a way that it was durable enough to survive what was to come, the flood. Concurrently (at the same time of building the Ark) he had to get all the supplies to sustain life while enduring the hardship of the weather. To complete the project Noah had to stock the supplies, select all the animals while also preparing his family. The Bible does not provide a time line as to how long it took Noah to finalize the craft, but one can imagine it took quite some time to accomplish each of these feats.

Then came the flood. During the time Noah and the Ark's contents were at sea, Noah was responsible for the safety of what was gathered on board. While the Bible does not say how he maintained the Ark, one could think that Noah and his family worked many hours taking care of the animals, and keeping the Ark afloat. After forty days and forty nights the rain stopped. It was said the earth was flooded for 150 days. On the seventeenth day of the seventh month the Ark came to rest on the mountains of Ararat. After a little while longer, God told Noah it was safe for him, his family and all animals to leave the Ark. Through the use of the magnificent refuge, the Ark, Noah completed his mission! All the precious items God wanted to come off the Ark at the end of the flood, came off.

How important is it to certify the customer receives exactly what was ordered? One would think that after the Ark was built and the contents gathered, the job would be done, right? No. Ensuring required items requested or needed make it to the final point of destination and in good condition is extremely important. Have you ever purchased a product and when received the packaging was damaged? Product damage can come from many sources; material packing process, originating business shipping process, shipping process, destination process, etc. Each item listed contains some sort of transportation. Whether it is shipped directly from the production line or if the shipping service picks it up from a central storage location. Some aspects of the shipping process have a core competency requirement. That requirement being transportation. The overall transport of a product is potential for waste. Meaning that every time a product is touched, whether during the production process or shipping process, there is potential for unnecessary item movement to enter into the process. This is a reason why companies take considerable time identifying a products critical path of delivery throughout the supply chain. Basically, a critical path is the longest sequence of activities an item needs to complete on time for the project to complete on its due date. With that concept in mind, it is important to see that Noah's job was not only to build the Ark, but to also arrange for safe delivery of the contents in the Ark.

Building the Ark took a considerable amount of time and resources to complete. During that time, Noah was responsible for maintaining focus and the right equipment and material were prepared to be installed at the appropriate time. This coordination of resources provided for a smooth transition between project phases. A project phase is when a project is broken into sections. This sectioning allows for better planning and aids with keeping the project in perspective, i.e. eating an elephant one bite at a time. How is delivery handled during modern times?

A modern-day company that utilized Focus On The Customer to build and expand was Walgreens. Over time, their strategy shifted from focusing on the store to utilizing data and customer preferences to provide forecasts of what is needed to meet customer demands. Walgreens strategy now is to maintain advantage throughout their supply chain through product positioning and planning to ensure the right product is predominantly showcased at the right time. An example of this is when a big winter storm is forecasted in a region of the United States. The company will place salt and snow removal supplies in predominant locations throughout the store so customers can easily find them. Founded in 1901 the company's vision is to be America's most-loved pharmacy-led health, well-being and beauty company. To be successful and consistent throughout the organization, Walgreens incorporated value chains to ensure customer needs were met.[6]

A Value Chain is comprised of activities a company takes to add value to their product or service. This concept contains both primary activities and secondary activities. Primary Activities include steps that must be accomplished to be successful. Secondary Activities are parts of the value chain that either support or enhance primary activities.

Through analysis of Walgreens' business model from suppliers to when the customer checks out at a store register, the company has developed a reliable process focused on adding value through well-defined systematic activities.[7] There has been significant value chain focused research completed. Throughout the one hundred years it took Noah to build the Ark, one value chain he would have worked with is how the building materials were prepared and staged to ensure a streamlined ship building process. If Noah did not have some sort of organization pertaining to how the ship was to be built, he most likely would have never completed the project.

Another fact about this event is, not only does the Jewish, Christian, and Islamic religion mention a great flood, but there are at least another ten cultures or religions mentioning a great flood occurring as well. Those are: Egyptian,

Greek, Hindu, Chinese, English, Polynesian, Mexican, Peruvian, Native American, and Greenland.[8] In addition to this, there are ancient writings dating back to before the nineteenth century B.C. mentioning a flood. One artifact was an ancient Sumerian stone tablet containing ancient text about a great flood.[9]

While it may be considered rare, having a customer who knows exactly what they want is extremely helpful with identifying project milestone completions. We can observe a lot that can be used today from the story of Noah's Ark. This story begins with God selecting a project lead. He (God) took time to lay out the details of what Noah was to do, how much material he was going to need, along with how he was to design the inside of the Ark. Additionally, God didn't just say, go get some animals, He was specific enough to identify the right kind and number of animals that were to be placed on the Ark.

From Noah's perspective, when working on any project, a project manager has to remain focused on the desired specifications of his customer. Importantly, meet customer deadline delivering a quality product. Just as Noah completed this project by meeting specific expectations and timelines, a project lead must remain true to the fact, that the desires of the customer are to take precedence as much as practical. When looking at the Ark, as it was laid out in stages that one can identify and see there was a need to confirm each stage of the project was successfully completed. Beginning with the identification of material needs and completing with all the Ark's contents successfully and safely leaving it after the flood ended.

It would have been easy to see, when God told him what was going to happen, Noah may have said something like, this is crazy building such a structure out of faith. But as we will continue to see, the Bible is full of examples of people taking leaps of faith to accomplish the impossible. What steps do you take to prepare your heart for receiving God?

Chapter Reflection:

1. How much do we need to take ownership of our lives? How much do we leave to God's control?
2. What methods do you think Noah took to ensure the Ark was built of high quality?
   a. Discuss what quality means to you. What methods do you take to ensure high quality materials?
3. Whether driving people to an event, or carrying cargo in your car, what steps do you take to protect the people and/or the cargo to ensure safe delivery?
4. What are your thoughts on the fact many different religions and other traditions discuss a great flood?
5. Noah took a leap of faith, trusting God to provide everything he needed to accomplish this monumental task. Based off how the pre-flood culture is described; do you feel you are standing in the boat or standing out in the world?

BRICKS WITHOUT STRAW

Psalm 100:5 (NIV)
For the Lord is good and his love endures forever; his faithfulness continues through all generations.

Before we go any farther, please take a moment and see if you can say "LET MY PEOPLE GO!" like Charlton Heston did in his Golden Globe winning performance in the movie, The Ten Commandments. If you don't know what I am talking about, check it out. Hear his passion, and desire in that one statement. Feel his passion as he says "Let my People go," while reading this chapter.

It is extremely important to provide resources and support necessary to a job. An important aspect to completing projects is focusing on minimizing the amount of frustration a worker endures to complete assigned tasks. After surviving four hundred and thirty years of captivity, let's begin with the examination of the Israelites and their exodus from Egypt. It took Moses adapting different strategies and then God having to send ten plagues to change Pharaoh's mind. The spotlight of this chapter highlights one aspect of the Israelites plight, "bricks without straw."

This story started when Moses went to the Pharaoh of Egypt to ask him to allow the Israelites to take a weekend to worship God. As a result of Moses' request, Pharaoh told his supervisors to stop providing straw to the brick makers and to be tougher on the Israelites. Pharaoh's action had multiple negative effects on the brick making process. The effect of not allowing straw was a key turning point in the Israelites decision to leave Egypt. By not listening to workers and eliminating a previously supplied critical ingredient in the brick making process Pharaoh had a significant impact both to the process and worker. This impact was not only witnessed in the quality of the product but also in the time to produce. Morale of the ones producing the product would also be drastically impacted. In this case, the product was bricks.

Before we try discussing the brick making process and Moses' actions to save the Israelites, let's start by discovering who Moses was. At the time Moses was born, there was a large population of Israelites in Egypt. The Pharaoh was worried about what may happen if they were to try to fight back over his oppression. Or, what if Israelites formed an alliance with an enemy. Due to this worry, the Pharaoh said, "Behold, the people of Israel are too many and too mighty for us. Come, let us deal shrewdly with them." So, the overseers were told to afflict Israelites with heavy burdens. But, the more the Israelites were oppressed, the more they multiplied. When the Pharaoh found this out, he ordered his men to kill all male babies by throwing them in the Nile river. Now let's return to Moses' story.[1]

Moses' mother saved him from being killed by hiding him for three months. As he grew, she realized she had to do something else to ensure he wasn't killed by the Pharaoh's order. She placed him in a basket at the time when the

Pharaoh's daughter would see him and take him as her own. Because the Pharaoh's daughter found him in water, she named him Moses. Due to Pharaoh's daughter taking Moses, he was able to grow up in royalty. Once a man, Moses saw how badly his people were being mistreated. Ultimately Moses killed an Egyptian because of how cruelly he was beating an Israelite.[2]

After killing the Egyptian, Moses fled to Midian. While in hiding, for approximately forty years, Moses married Zipporah and they had a child. They named their child Gershom. Back in Egypt, Pharaoh continued to oppress the Israelites. In time, the Pharaoh died and a new Pharaoh ascended into power. During this time, the Israelites continued to pray, crying out for help. God heard them and appointed Moses to help in their plight. History tells us, Moses had grown comfortable with his life outside of Egypt. This was when God spoke to Moses through the burning bush. After listening to what God wanted Moses to do, Moses replied, "Who am I that I should go to Pharaoh and bring the children of Israel out of Egypt?" But, like the stories before us and the ones yet to be discussed, Moses spoke with God to make sure he had God's plan together when he went back. God also let Moses know that the men who were seeking his life were dead.[3]

Then, by faith, Moses set off to free the Israelites in Egypt. Throughout this time, Moses knew he was not going to just go in to Egypt, and tell the Israelites why he was there and they would just blindly follow him. Clearly understand Moses knew that not only was he going to have to persuade Pharaoh, he was also going to have to change the Israelite minds as well. During the returning trip, while also confronting his own doubts, Moses asked God a question about how to prove that He was with him when challenged. God spoke to him to reassure Moses that he was ready to handle this journey. What Moses must have felt due to these heavy burdens he would have placed on himself. Thinking about why he left Egypt and wondering if people would follow him. Prior to him arriving in Egypt, Moses had to work through this fear because when he arrived, he had to be confident. Ready to face adversity from both the Pharaoh and the Israelites. Due to his fears and lack of confidence in his ability to persuade, God let Moses' brother Aaron speak for him. With Aaron by his side, Moses was prepared to accomplish his assignment. Because the Israelites were oppressed for so long, Moses and Aaron's task of changing minds would have been extremely tough. So, with God's support, Moses started with small acts of persuasion during an elder meeting to garner their attention and prove he was there to help.

In his book, Leading Change, Dr. John P. Kotter talked about using an eight-stage process to create major change. The first stage was, Establishing a Sense of Urgency. During this stage, the challenge is developing a sense of purpose with excitement to support the change. Working to develop cooperation and a compelling mission, one is able to get the people and resources needed to accomplish the goal.[4] Moses had started this change when he and Aaron met with the elders. During this meeting he showed them he was serious. By the act of turning his staff into a snake, the elders realized Moses and Aaron were telling the divine truth. After this meeting with the elders, Moses went to Pharaoh and made his request to allow the Israelites three days so they could go in to the wilderness to worship God.

In response, Pharaoh decided he needed to take his oppression to a new level. Beginning with instructing his supervisors to stop providing straw for bricks. With straw not being provided, the Israelites were still required to meet their daily brick making quota. Additionally, by allowing Israelites to leave, the time away may have provided the them additional energy to maybe cause an uprising. Having been oppressed for four hundred years, the Israelites had been praying for positive change. Through Moses and Aaron, they were going to get that change. Having been in captivity for four-hundred years, the Israelites probably didn't know what a better life looked like. Culture is based on how people interact and develop personally through learned behaviors. Taking steps to provide the Israelites with a new, fresh vision would most likely have been met with mixed feelings; however, in the end would have aided getting everyone on board.[5]

Returning to the book Leading Change, Dr. John P. Kotter laid out a plan on how to execute change. Initially with focused small wins, change happens when employees begin to implement new practices and behaviors in their daily activities. Dr. Kotter continued by discussing how Change Leaders need to be prepared for detractors and dissension. When the timing is right, even with added resistance to change; further depending on and communicating the significance of the change and how change is instituted is key for success. When getting a few employees onboard is fine, in the beginning. While over time winning others. Additionally, there will be some who are not prepared to go all the way with the change. Being a Change Leader, it is important to remain prepared for this pushback during change. Preparation in anticipating adversity will aid with leading a successful change effort.[6] Throughout his return to Egypt, Moses discussed this challenge with God. Taking an approach to include his brother Aaron and meet with Elders was an important aspect of incorporating a change strategy and accomplishing the goal of getting Israelites freed.

So, what was Pharaoh risking by letting the Israelites go for three days? Pharaoh knew he would lose if Israelites were allowed to leave for three days and they didn't return. Who would complete his projects? A document used to record daily brick delivery and quota by foremen was the Louvre Leather Roll. Based off this document, each foreman was required to have produced two-thousand bricks a day. The foremen oversaw Israelite brick makers. If Israelites sole purpose was to make a minimum of 200 bricks per day (this number is hypothetical) and they were wanting to leave for three days, how would the foremen meet their quota? On the low end, say there were one thousand Israelites making bricks. That would be two hundred thousand bricks per day. Combined for the lost production over the three days, that would be a missed opportunity for 600,000 bricks being made.[7] Looking solely at the numbers, one could see why Pharaoh did not support the loss of production for three days. On top of this, add the fact that the brick makers also had to add in gathering straw to their process of making bricks. Why was putting straw in bricks so important? It has been identified that straw was used to make bricks stronger and durable to stand the test of time (Bricks without straw crumbled easily). Incorporating the added amount of time for Israelites to gather straw, would most likely add at least another hour to two hours to the workday in addition to the added physical exertion of pulling straw from the ground. Overall, that would be an added twenty to forty thousand hours of work added each day.

In making his decision to stop providing straw, Pharaoh probably did not place much thought into what the added production processes would do to the Israelites. While it may have seemed insignificant, when a work flow is modified to add additional steps, there are both intended and unintended consequences. The intended consequences may mean less down time, or slack in the overall process time when it came to incorporating the straw in the bricks. With this added step, workers may have been tempted to either not put straw in the bricks or put less than they normally would. This would have been a direct impact to the quality of the product being produced.

Looking at the situation from the Israelites point of view, one can see how they were at their physical and emotional breaking point. Drastic action needed to be taken to improve their lives. Delving further into this, one can see how important it is to provide workers with the right tools to be successful in their jobs. Whether the tool is more education or an instrument, like a trowel. Utilizing an employee focused strategy provides for a learning and growing environment. When additional items are added to a workflow, not only is there potential for worker frustration in being given more work, there is also a level of quality that may be compromised. The Book, <u>Bringing Out The Best in People</u> by Aubrey Daniels is a good resource to further dig into developing a culture of growth through positive reinforcement and employee centered strategies. Dr. Daniels' book is focused on working to develop a stable workforce through clear expectations and having an open communication channel. The strategies he explained has provided for improvements not only with leaders and followers, but also in the quality of the product being produced.[8]

Chapter Reflection:

1. Discuss how the Israelite captivity had been prophesied. Refer to Genesis 15:13 and Acts 7:6
2. Prior to Moses standing up for Israelites, do you think Israelites were adjusting to the abuse they were experiencing?
    a. Discuss impacts of the situation when Pharaoh tried to change Israelite behavior through negative reinforcement.
    b. How would employees respond to this type of treatment today?
3. Thinking of today's work environments, how would you respond to your boss taking away a key resource of getting the job done and you having to do it all by yourself. Below are conversation starters, not an all-inclusive list. Also discuss how this could impact a company's core competencies.
    a. The purchasing department is taken away and you had to order and accept all your supplies.
    b. You, the employee, now has to perform all machine preventative maintenance; calibration, simple maintenance speed up process since

operators don't have to wait on maintenance people.
4. In his book, Bringing Out the Best in People, Aubrey Daniels states, "Breakthrough performance rarely occurs with negative reinforcement, but negative reinforcement does have application in business."
   a. Discuss when negative reinforcement may be warranted?
   b. Based on actions of the Pharaoh took against the Israelites, ask if, was negative reinforcement warranted when Moses asked the Pharaoh to grant the Israelites three days to go pray?

DAVID AND GOLIATH

1 Kings 20:11 NIV
"One who puts on his armor should not boast like one who takes it off."

There are times when too much or too little can be inserted into a problem. Which in the end prevents the problem from being solved due to either the increase in scope of work or not enough support to complete it. This chapter examines who King David was before his famous rendezvous with Goliath. We will also look at what it may take to identify that the right tools are selected for the task at hand ensuring the final result is accomplished without pouring too many resources into it.

At the time Samuel came to anoint the next king, David was the youngest of eight brothers. While his father, Jesse, was introducing Samuel to his older brothers, David was in the fields taking care of the sheep. When Samuel had looked at all of his brothers, he asked Jesse if there were any other children. Jesse said yes and sent for David. When Samuel saw David, the Lord confirmed he would be the next king, so Samuel anointed him. There is more background to this story, but the focus of this chapter is on how David confronted one of the biggest challenges in his life.[1]

A short time after Samuel visited David and his family, three of his brothers and the Israelite army found themselves in a standoff against the Philistines. The Israelites were being intimidated by a man named Goliath, a Philistine, who challenged them for forty days. Every day he would come out and challenge the Israelites to send their best fighter to fight him. If Goliath lost, the Philistines would become the Israelites slaves, and vice versa. Goliath was quite large in physical stature, and heavily armed. Any normal person could see the reasoning why not one person would want to challenge the mighty Goliath in a one on one fight.[2] Goliath had put on all his armor he felt he needed to beat any threat. He was carrying a sword, as well as putting on armor. He had other defenses including a shield bearer in front of him. Goliath was very well prepared. Goliath's though he was invincible and could defeat any enemy. Conversely when David put on all the armor and gear the Israelites felt he would need to fight Goliath but he did not feel comfortable with this gear and did not think he would be able to win if he wore his armor to the fight.

Having more gear than needed to address a problem can end up getting in one's way. Companies spend a lot of time researching and identifying what the right balance of tools and software programs an employee needs to use to be successful. There are times the company is successful, and times they are not. When a company does not invest in ensuring the right tool or software program is available, there is potential for selecting the wrong tools which can impact the result. Too many unused tools rarely being used can clutter the storage closet. Consider meeting with the users to engage their opinions to determine what is needed to successfully complete the task. Engagement of all stakeholders will aid with minimizing frustrations due to tools not being readily available when needed.³

Now back to David and Goliath. They both had been in battles before. Goliath had fought battles with other armies since he was young. David had fought lions and bears protecting his sheep when he was young. Looking at the different training perspectives of experience from fighting in many battles, may have explained why Goliath carried so much. Each weapon and piece of gear had a specific role ensuring Goliath was victorious when facing adversaries. David on the other hand, carried gear that was light and small so he could better catch and kill his adversaries such as lions and bears. Over time, after being scratched or bitten a couple of times, he also would have learned that it was better to fight one of these animals from a distance instead of engaging at close range. The animal would have most likely been stronger and quicker than him. They could have easily overcome David at close range. Having become an expert at long distance fighting would have aided in competing with Goliath and would have provided his best chance for a successful outcome (winning).

Using one stone, David took care of a very big problem. Sometimes less is more when it comes to dealing with a big problem. Contrasting with today's business world, there are examples of companies dedicating more resources than needed and are left with either ending the project before completion or having to spend more funds than allocated to complete it. That is why it is extremely important to fully understand the many aspects of a project. It is necessary to confirm that the amount of resources are available when needed. Examine and identify items critical to the project completion. Having a list identified at the beginning provides key information to develop a reliable critical path to success. A well-defined path would not only contain the most direct avenue to completing the project but would also contain those nice to haves to ensure everything is captured. A reason for also capturing nice to haves is once the project is under way, there may be a time when these nice to haves could become critical to the project's success.

The example of David and Goliath places a man having to directly confront another man who was much stronger and more experienced in combat. There comes a time in one's life where the easy decision is to keep taking care of the sheep and living the routine life of warding off predators. Fortunately, David made the decision to trust God and went in to battle. There are times in life where a problem is bigger than any we have ever confronted. The easy decision may be to not take the lead, just support the effort, choosing to not go for it and to avoid the confrontation. The other choice, the more difficult choice, is to embrace ownership of the lead role and face the adversaries before you head on. When has this happened in your life? Was the result worth it?

What resources are needed to address a challenge and develop a plan to identify what it will take to be successful. Depending on scale, one can incorporate different strategies. Examples of established process improvement strategies one could employ are: DMAIC, 5S, Lean, and Kaizen. Each of these strategies has its own dynamic that provides for one to be successful whether the project may focus on either process improvements or area reorganization. Please be mindful of the amount of physical resources needed.

Sometimes it is easy to get more than we need such as extra staff to support infrastructure or purchasing extra materials, etc. The one who manages must remain committed to evaluating required resources to stay as efficient and effective as possible in the project. Tying up more resources than needed may have a negative impact as well on fiscal cost. At times, when too many resources are committed, other operations within the company may suffer.

It is understandable that a person may not be at a point to fully take advantage of analytical strategies. If that is the case, it is recommended to find someone who is knowledgeable to provide the analysis to aid in preventing unnecessary financial cost, and the acquisition of unneeded resources. Recognize the challenge of analytical options one has when working on a problem. Whether the correct tool is physical like a hammer, a scientific instrument (Used to measure, track, or record an item of importance), or work process planning, communication, deliberate implementation of processes will always aid with being successful.[4]

Chapter Reflection:

1. How important was it for David to have a different perspective when going into battle with Goliath? Discuss
2. When David was confronted with having to battle a different adversary, man instead of animal, did he believe he could beat Goliath on his own?
    a. What/who was he depending on to bring him through the battle?
3. It was apparent Goliath had won many battles and

was confident in his capabilities to win the next one, regardless of whom ever from the Israelites sent forward. Discuss the importance of remembering verse 1 Kings 20:11.

   a. As we go through our daily lives, what tactic or strategies can we put in place to remember this verse?

4. Discuss a time in your life when you faced a Goliath sized problem.

   a. How did you handle it?

   b. What would you do differently?

SOLOMON'S TEMPLE

Proverbs 1:7 NIV
The fear of the L<small>ORD</small> is the beginning of knowledge; fools despise wisdom and instruction.

This chapter focuses on utilizing outside resources and partnering with more experienced resources to support the completion of a project. As King Solomon inventoried his available resources to build God's temple, he recognized there was another more qualified person he should contact who was better at providing the much-needed resource, wood. While King Solomon had the manpower to provide the project. We learn from history that focusing on one's core competencies and partnering with others to build a project is a tactic that has been used throughout time. The supply chain has multiple actors, with each actor providing a resource and competency the other does not have.

    Core competencies are recognized when a company takes time to identify their internal strengths and are moving to ensure they are aligned with customer needs. Losing focus on core competencies will cause a business to eventually fail. Remember focus and developing critical points of reminders is why a company exists and must be accomplished to ensure continued success of any enterprise. Without focus, excessive resources and critical time will be lost.[1]

King Solomon, son of King David, took over the kingdom and committed to completing the temple to the Lord. Knowing what resources, he needed to complete the temple, Solomon made an agreement with Hiram, king of Tyre. In his proposal, Solomon wanted Hiram's country to supply wood. With this agreement in place, Solomon began building the temple by sending the labor to Hiram to cut and send timbers. Thirty thousand laborers were identified and sent in one-month waves of ten thousand men. The strategy for the laborers was to have them go to Lebanon, support tree harvesting for one month and then spend two months at home. While it is not said what the laborers did while at home for two months, this rotational strategy most likely provided a healthy labor force. King Solomon recognized the need for laborers to rest. By keeping them fresh, the overall production would have had little variation due to worker fatigue.[2]

Identifying and developing a sound rotation program takes time to ensure multiple items have been addressed. The first question is, what aspects of the workforce are going to be impacted. This looks at identifying what skills are needed and how will they be used. Developing a standard rotation plan may seem to be easy for a company to implement. However, not all assignments will have the same depth or duration. If the planned amount of time a worker is away is too short, then it will cost the company added expenses to either extend the assignment because the assignment cannot be completed or send another resource to complete the task. On the other hand, if it is too long, then there is a risk of workers wasting time and being unproductive. To anticipate this, analyze what would be the best way to initiate a task with focus on the step by step task to be completed. Consider benchmarking to identify how long it took similar projects to be completed. Additionally, a plan needs to be in place pertaining to where the material will be assembled when the assignment is complete. One step further it would be a good idea to have milestones, or check-in points. This will aid in keeping the project duration realistic and provide for the worker to be more involved in the overall process. Finally, adding some flexibility to the assignment will aid by ensuring the project is completed both on time and minimizing waste within the total project.[3]

At home, Solomon placed one man in charge of the workforce. His name was Adoniram, also known as Hiram Abif. The workforce consisted of: seventy thousand carriers, eighty thousand stone cutters, and thirty-three hundred foremen to supervise work. Looking at labor segmentation, it is clear there was a deliberate reason why there were more stone cutters than carriers. Most likely it took a longer period of time to cut the stone than carry them to their final destination.

Having tactics to develop and foster a workforce with broad skills will aid in breaking through organizational silos. The overseer, master of the project, will aid in breaking through organizational silos. Many times, there is a need to have an established workforce segmentation program. While the overseer or master, will have knowledge, and skills to complete many tasks, the specialists are better suited to address detailed assignments. An example of a specialized group could be an organizations maintenance department. A maintenance department has specific, detailed knowledge of how to properly use specialized instruments and tools. They will also have the depth of knowledge to better handle those rare events. The generalist will have the overall knowledge to complete routine tasks, and may possess some detailed knowledge to address some rare events. However, when the rare events arise, the specialist (Maintenance department) is better trained to address it.[4]

Following God's decrees for temple specifications and strategies, Solomon completed the temple with a total project time of eleven years and eight months, seven of those years were spent actually building it. Let's look back at how the Bible laid out this project. It started with specifics about how the building was to be designed and scope of work expectations. An example of one expectation was in a Bible verse stating, "In building the temple, only blocks dressed at the quarry were used, and no hammer, chisel or any other iron tool was heard at the temple site while it was being built."[5]

Project duration has the potential to be a variable which can determine whether a project will succeed or fail. Establishing a key point of management, a project lead, will aid with ensuring important aspects are not missed and the project stays on schedule. Beginning with a project plan, the project lead makes decisions and navigates through plan details for a successful conclusion.

Solomon went to great lengths to develop a relationship that was advantageous for both parties. In the end, Solomon completed his project and King Hiram increased his land. While they both had issues they had to work through during this time due to King Hiram being disappointed with the land he received, communication was important for project success. Finally, flexibility and follow through remains to be a key aspect of project success. Beginning with asking God for wisdom, Solomon grew his kingdom and completed what God had asked him to do.

Chapter Reflection:

1. Why do you think Solomon prayed for wisdom?
2. Instead of trying to do everything by himself, Solomon asked Hiram, King of Tyre to help with providing resources to build the temple. When have you ever trusted someone else to complete something alongside you?
   a. How were individual expectations handled?
   b. What was the outcome? i.e. was the project or adventure successful?
   c. If the other individual did not live up to expectations, how did you handle it?
3. The amount of time it took to build the temple was eleven years. What strategies and tactics would you use to remain focused on the end product?
   a. What about strategies to minimize project scope creep (allowing additional work, not directly related to original project to become part of the project)?

CLEANING THE TEMPLE

Psalm 51:10 NIV
Create in me a clean heart, O God, and
renew a right spirit within me.

A method for maintaining and cleaning the facility must be developed when a project is complete. This maintenance plan aids in keeping areas, or buildings clean and clear of clutter. Once King Solomon completed the temple and the palace, he and his generation became distracted. They began worshiping other gods and filling the temple with items that were not holy to God. Over time the original purpose for building the temple, to worship and praise God was lost. Years later Hezekiah became king when he was twenty-nine years old and within his first year he started to clean the temple.[1] What we will cover in this chapter was completed thousands of years ago, but closely aligns with a current day Lean strategy called 5S. Before we go further into King Hezekiah's strategy on cleaning the temple, let's get a common understanding of 5S.

5S was developed to be a process improvement tool focused not only on cleaning an area, but also standardizing and sustaining work practices to ensure improvements are maintained. 5S stands for: Sort, Set in order,

Shine, Standardize, and Sustain. Utilizing 5S aids with workplace standardization through establishing a visual workplace, i.e. visual job aids, signs, visual guidance on proper item placement, or material refill lines. Additionally, it ensures the area does not return to its original condition by establishing post 5S evolution guidance.[2]

5S defined:

Sort – Remove any unnecessary items, i.e. broken, or no longer applicable to area.
Set in Order – Organize remaining items by arranging and grouping based on item type.
Shine – Clean area, including all equipment and related materials.
Standardize – Develop a schedule to be used to ensure area remains clutter free.
Sustain – Continue to internalize the first four S's to ensure area is properly maintained.

During his first year, Hezekiah worked with the Levites to clean the temple and re-set everything back in order. Because he was distracted, not only from his responsibilities, but also in his following of God, Solomon allowed the temple to become a storage place for other gods and rituals and it accumulated items that did not belong there. This falling away from the reason God's Temple was constructed continued over generations. The tipping point came when King Ahaz closed the doors to God's temple, and placed alters throughout the city so sacrifices could be made to other gods. The following focuses on what King Hezekiah,

King Ahaz's son, did to return the temple Solomon had built to worship God.³

Beginning in the first month of his reign, King Hezekiah assembled the Levites and explained his expectations of what was to be accomplished. They removed all items not appropriate for the temple and replaced the idolatry with items suitable for worshipping God. The reason for using Levites for this task dates to the days of Moses when they were put in charge of the tabernacle of the covenant of God's law. Included were all its furnishings and everything belonging to it.⁴ So, the Levites started by consecrating themselves. They then removed all items that should not be in the temple. This activity can be related to the first step of the 5S process improvement model, Sort. Following this, while putting holy items in place, they cleansed and placed the alter for burnt offerings, along with all its requisite utensils and the alter for leavened bread. These activities fit with the second and third steps of the 5S process, Set in Order and Shine. Upon completion they resumed the recognized practices established by God through King David. This can be related to the fourth step in 5S, Standardize. This cleansing process took sixteen days. When the process was complete, the Levites reported their progress to King Hezekiah.

When projects are complete, no matter how big the task was to accomplish, a celebration should be held to show both what has been accomplished and allow members the opportunity to celebrate their successes. Upon being informed by the Levites God's temple was ready, King Hezekiah gathered the city officials and had the Levites sacrifice animals and present burnt offerings. He stationed the Levites in the temple with musical instruments. Following this ceremony, King Hezekiah sent out invitations throughout Israel inviting people to come to the temple to celebrate Passover. It turns out, this celebration was so big it lasted seven days longer than the originally planned seven-day celebration. Encouraged by what had been accomplished, attendees returned to their cities and destroyed the idols placed to worship other gods. God's temple and all applicable rituals and ceremonies were re-established. This final activity fits the fifth step in the 5S process, Sustain.

Besides having a clean work area and standardized process, there are other benefits of utilizing 5S methodologies. Some added benefits include: improved safety, higher equipment availability, improved employee morale, and better image of the customer. Beginning with safety, a 5S project modifies unkept areas into being well organized and decluttered. This will free an area from potential safety hazards such as items laying on the floor or unsecure stacks of boxes. Completed 5S projects provide for the desired foundation of any work area. Higher equipment availability could also be achieved through implementing periodic preventative maintenance programs. Additionally, employee moral will improve when attention is placed on improving work areas by removing potentially frustrating messy conditions and organizing to reduce unnecessary frustrations. There is also a positive impact in customer relations. Having areas maintained and clutter free, the customer will have an added level of confidence on the product being received.[5]

Chapter Reflection:
After reading below Bible verses, answer below questions.
2 Chronicles 29:24-27,

"Ahaz gathered together the furnishings from the temple of God and cut them in pieces. He shut the doors of the Lord's temple and set up altars at every street corner in Jerusalem. In every town in Judah he built high places to burn sacrifices to other gods and aroused the anger of the Lord, the God of his ancestors.

1. The other events of his reign and all his ways, from beginning to end, are written in the book of the kings of Judah and Israel. Ahaz rested with his ancestors and was buried in the city of Jerusalem, but he was not placed in the tombs of the kings of Israel. And Hezekiah his son succeeded him as king."
   a. How do you think knowing his father was not placed in the tombs of the kings of Israel impacted King Hezekiah?
   b. Would witnessing the above event have provided the motivation for King Hezekiah to reopen God's temple and re-establish rituals/ceremonies focused on praising God?
2. Do you think King Hezekiah received any resistance when he started to implement his plan of cleaning God's temple?
3. How do you think the Levites felt when King Hezekiah made his request?
   a. Do you think they were happy to get the request,

or would they have pushed back before accepting the assignment?
4. Think about a time when you worked on a similar project, whether improving an area at work or home, to answer the following:
   a. Would utilizing 5S methodologies mentioned in this chapter have improved the outcome?
   b. How does having an established method for completing related tasks make it easier to communicate with all involved?

REACHING THE MASSES

Matthew 7:24 NIV
Everyone then who hears these words of
mine and does them will be like a wise man
who built his house on the rock.

When Jesus began his ministry, he used love, miracles and parables to relate God's unconditional love. Prior to Jesus coming, God's messages had been delivered through prophets and kings. Upon His arrival and through His teaching, Jesus made it possible for the word of God to be spread to the masses. The desire for people to continue His ministry is illustrated multiple times throughout the New Testament. One example is when he came to the fishermen and told them to drop their nets, he will make them fishers of men.[1]

Fishermen using nets gave an added advantage of being able to bring in a large quantity of fish with less effort than catching them one at a time. During Jesus' time fish were a primary source of protein. The Sea of Galilee is a fresh water lake and was the center for many different communities located around the lake. The three types of fish fishermen caught were: tilapia (St. Peter's fish), carp, and catfish. Fishermen sold their fish around local markets. The Jewish community believed catfish were unclean due to it not having fins and scales. So, they wouldn't go to waste, catfish were sold to the Greeks.[2]

Fishing was a lucrative industry during biblical times. Fishermen fished at night to prevent fish from swimming around the nets because of the material (flax or linen) used to make the nets. Present day fishermen do not have that problem due to the use of nylon to make nets. Nylon makes the nets harder for fish to see. Utilizing a small number of boats, usually three, fishermen would coordinate hauling the large nets full of fish into the boats. This was a physically demanding job that required a lot of hard work. This process of catching fish was completed multiple times throughout the night. By morning the volume of fish brought in was around a half ton. Once on shore, the boat and fishing equipment were put back in a condition so the process could be repeated the next night. In parallel to getting the boat ready, fish were sorted and prepared for sale. By the way, a byproduct of the fishing industry involved taking fish entrails and fish too small to sell, then using salt and time spent in the sun to create a sauce called garum. This garum was used as an additive during most meals.[2]

When Jesus began his ministry, he brought a new perspective for people to worship God. Besides being our Savior, there are many applications today in what Jesus did for the world. How effective do you think Jesus would have been if he came to earth and did not spend time relating God's love but only told people about God, the personality or only talked about historical biblical events. When Jesus told the fishermen to drop their nets, they responded and followed Him. Jesus not only touched lives on the individual level but as his ministry grew, He impacted people on a large scale. On the individual level, Jesus focused on showing how much God loved them through telling parables and performing miracles. Jesus found success in relating God's desire through meeting with people on a one on one or small group basis, in addition to delivering messages to large audiences. Taking an individual approach brings faster relationship building and more individualized solutions. Jesus knew he was going to be on earth for a short period of time. Therefore, he knew that he needed to spread his message through believers and large crowds.

Jesus tailored his messages to be relational on a large scale. Basically, what he said two thousand years ago is still applicable today. Building off his ability to reach large audiences one can utilize those principles and apply to how modern businesses operate. Like the fishermen with nets, there is an inherent added efficiency business receive with mass producing instead of using a one piece at a time strategy. There are many lessons learned from this analogy, but the first lesson to consider is how to not limit capabilities by thinking small.

While mass production has been around in some form throughout the centuries, it came into prominence in the early twentieth century. An example of this was with the advances of automobile manufacturing and the manufacturing of other consumer products. Over time a company's mass-producing activities not only configured their processes to be efficient, but also worked to educate a workforce to continually look for methods to identify efficiencies. Mass production is focused on providing large quantities of products at lower costs. In 1909, Henry Ford brought this production strategy home with his famous statement, "Any customer can have a car painted any color that he wants so long as it is black." It has been identified that a main reason for painting cars black was that black dried fast. It was also significantly cheaper to produce one color of car compared to cars painted in different colors.[3] Other examples of products that are currently mass produced include: mobile phones, computers, cars, kitchen appliances, etc.

The benefits of mass production include reduced labor costs, faster production rates and less cost per unit. In mass producing, there are varying degrees of automation. This automation provides for more pieces to get through the production process in an expeditious manner with work being more standardized. Remember an increased production rate allows for the cost per unit to go down because the time in process is reduced. The prime example is reduced labor costs. Reduced labor cost occurs when manufacturing processes are automated. The labor cost savings are attributed to the automation process reducing time to handle the product. When evaluating the benefits of mass production, the cost benefit is achieved when working to mass produce the same item. If additional customization to a product is needed, mass production may not be the best method to use.[4]

Disadvantages of mass production include:

- Less variety in products being produced,
- Wasted equipment downtime, and
- No assurance

When mass producing a product, the cost to change out machines to produce another product may be expensive.

A strategy one company can use to aid in minimizing the cost to change out equipment during product changes include: product batching and SMED (Single Minute Exchange of Dies). SMED is a strategy of reducing equipment change over time so the next product line can begin operations in a short period of time. The long-term objective of SMED is zero time to changeover equipment.[5]

Wasted resources can create another disadvantage to mass producing. A piece of equipment may become defective, potentially leading to a large amount of product being defective. In his book, The Toyota Way, Dr. Jeffrey Liker talks about a system Toyota used to quickly identify production problems called Andon. Andon incorporates the use of flags or lights to alert workers there is a problem. Through rapid identification of equipment defects, the production line can be stopped, problems addressed, and the production line resumed in a short amount of time.[6]

The underlying goal of mass production is to be able to reach the largest customer base. Mass production is analogous to mass communications. Mass communications focuses on delivering a message to a large group of people. When Jesus performed the Sermon on the Mount, see Matthew 5, he delivered one message to a large group. His message was applicable to all in attendance and provided the foundation for Christians. In 393, St. Augustine wrote the following about this sermon,

> "If anyone will piously and soberly consider the sermon which our Lord Jesus Christ spoke on the mount, as we read it in the Gospel according to Matthew, I think that he will find in it, so far as

regards the highest morals, a perfect standard of the Christian life."[7]

In this message Jesus focused on how one should live and treat others. The Sermon on the Mount went into detail with Jesus covering a wide range of important aspects of life. Another takeaway from this is how Jesus was showing his disciples what it was going to take to spread God's word after he ascended into heaven. The knowledge and wisdom Jesus gave freely, so must believers be willing to do the same. As Jesus continued his message of the sermon, he talked about being the salt of the earth and what happens when salt loses its taste. Continuing, Jesus explained how believers are the light of the world. As believers we cannot hide the talents with which we have been blessed.[8]

Matthew 5:14-16 NIV:

> "You are the light of the world. A city set on a hill cannot be hidden. Nor do people light a lamp and put it under a basket, but on a stand, and it gives light to all in the house. In the same way, let your light shine before others, so that they may see your good works and give glory to your father who is in heaven."

Over time leaders of companies mass-producing products began to see this strategy was not entirely meeting customer needs. Businesses began to move from a product driven focus to a customer focused approach. This switch in process began to be termed as demassification. From demassification came mass customization. As customer needs evolved and began to take on a larger role in the production process, customer segmentation became more critical for businesses to grow. Mass customization focuses operations on a customer by customer basis. Which in turn better meets customer requirements.[9]

Toyota was a business that capitalized on a mass customization strategy. Emerging from WWII, Toyota took a more individualistic strategy because its market at the time was too small to justify mass producing cars. After touring Ford Company's automobile manufacturing line. Seeing how Ford mass produced cars, Taiichi Ohno (Toyota Plant Manager) developed a continuous flow process that provided Toyota the flexibility it needed to better meet customer needs. By developing a process proactive to customer needs, Toyota was able to provide customers more of what they wanted as well as reduce overall production costs. This cost reduction was achieved by reducing the amount of idle material sitting at different stages of the production process. The mass production strategy of working large amounts of product through the process in stages potentially creates a larger work in progress (WIP) inventory.[10]

The Dell Corporation is another example that uses mass customization processes to meet customer demands. Started in the early 1980's the founder, Michael Dell, developed methods to work both with customers and suppliers to develop a product that, like mass production, is less expensive, but does not have the excess inventory and bulk processes that comes with mass producing products. The Dell Corporation used a strategy called demand-pull. Utilizing this strategy, a customer can select the computer that best meets their needs. The Dell Corporation has the capability to then build and ship their products within twenty-four hours. To become this efficient and customer centric, Michael Dell spent time developing relationships with suppliers. Having a sound communication strategy with suppliers reduced lead times in getting needed parts to complete orders. By letting suppliers know of product requirements Dell Corporation suppliers were better able to forecast demands for their products.[11]

An ice company located in Northeast Tennessee, Harman Ice, is another example of taking mass production to the next step of working to meet customer needs. Harman Ice began in 1915 producing large blocks of ice and coal. The blocks of ice were delivered to customers houses and used to keep items cool in early refrigerators. This was prior to the mass production of electric refrigerators. The company adjusted its plan when electric refrigerators were mass produced and began selling crushed ice. As the years moved, the company focused on keeping technology current to ensure customer demands were being met. Today, Harman Ice can produce more than three hundred and fifty tons of ice a day. This turns into seventy thousand ten-pound packages. As technology has improved, the company has developed methods for customizing ice bags to meet customer needs. Having a capability to customize orders provides for a good mixture of mass producing and mass customization for the company.[12]

Beginning a journey with a sound foundation provides for the outcome to be successful. Foundation support should begin with an internal commitment to remain focused on learning more about God and how Jesus led by example. As a leader, implementing ideas, whether big or small, we must remain focused. When Jesus started his ministry, he began by developing relationships. Jesus started in small groups and then spread His message to large crowds. Consider this comparison to a business operation. Henry Ford brought to the world an efficient method to mass produce cars (large crowds). When he accomplished this feat, not only could the wealthy afford cars, but also the majority (masses) of the population could afford one. Based on the product being produced, a company can also tailor their strategy to best meet both operational and customer needs. Toyota and Dell designed production processes that were more responsive to customer needs. Harman Ice worked to maximize the customer experience through staying true with their founding principles in the production of ice and tailoring the experience to meet customer needs. Each method of production focused on an underlying principle of bringing the per unit cost down. This provides the foundation for a larger portion of the population opportunities to improve their lifestyles and daily lives.

Jesus held sermons focused on God and what following Him was all about. At the beginning of his ministry, during the wedding at Cana, Jesus performed his first miracle of turning water into wine. During the wedding the wine had run out and there was a need for more. While Jesus said His time had not come, he honored his mother's request and agreed to turn the water in six stone water jars into wine. Upon tasting it, the master of the feast complimented the bridegroom saying, "Everyone serves the good wine first, and when people have drunk freely, then the poor wine. But you have kept the good wine until now." Throughout his ministry Jesus performed many great miracles and was able to reach a large number of people who became His followers.[13]

Chapter Reflection:

1. What are you going to do with your lampstand, cover it, or let it shine?
2. What do you think the fishermen thought when they met Jesus and he told them to throw down their nets?
   a. How tough would it be for you to do the same? Leave everything and everyone you know to follow by faith?
3. Think of a time you had to deliver a message to others, how did you prepare to ensure your message was well delivered?
   a. What actions did you take to better relate the message so others could further internalize your message?
   b. How many meetings, or conversations have there been, where the message and delivery were so impersonal, you did not see get the point of the message being delivered?
4. Discuss how Jesus' message about being the light of the world, Matthew 5:14-16, resonates with you.
5. Jesus used his messages and miracles to reach large audiences. Over time his message extended to others through his disciples and followers (casting nets).
   a. At what point do we "drop our nets" and follow Jesus?

b. What actions should we take to grow our talents to ensure we don't try to hide them?
6. In reference to becoming "fishers of men", developing relationships and spreading God's word. What methods can you take to cast your net for Jesus?

STAYING FOCUSED

James 1:4 NIV
Let perseverance finish its work so that you may
be mature and complete, not lacking anything.

As we draw closer to the end of this book, it is important to remember that when completing a project, the effort of ensuring project gains must continue. Another dynamic of leadership enters that cannot be overlooked, examination after the project was completed. This chapter returns to King David and King Solomon. Both Kings completed monumental tasks to include the slaying of a giant, and to building God's temple. But what happened to these King's after they had conquered the lands and built the temple and palace? The Bible talks about them losing focus. The following will be a brief review of what they accomplished, and then a discuss what happened to them. Do you remember what God said at the end of the sixth day of creation? He said, "It is good." As we walk through this chapter, determine whether these individuals said "it is good" or "it is done."

KING DAVID

After King David killed Goliath, he built a strong empire that was feared by others. As time went by, King David lost focus and began to think more about taking care of himself than following through with God's promises. This was revealed when he remained at home when he sent his warriors off to battle. During their time away fighting King David saw a woman, Bathsheba bathing on the roof top. What King David, did started a long spiral down before he returns to God.

What does a person do when the battle is over to remain focused? Unfortunately for King David, by choosing to not go back into battle the sequence of events eventually led to the unfolding of negative outcomes for the kingdom he had built. The Bible tells of King David being successful at defeating the Arameans. We then see that King David lost focus and instead of going off to war to defeat the Ammonites, he stayed behind in the city, and sent his troops off without him. Since he did not have a campaign to lead, King David's mind and eyes started to drift to another thing, and that other thing turned out to be a beautiful woman, Bathsheba. The story continued with David trying to conceal his transgressions through deceit and even murder.[1]

Many of the process improvement and lean methodologies have incorporated stages that aids with keeping ones focused on the need to continue to maintain previous economic gains. One example is the Six Sigma DMAIC methodologies. The first four letters stand for; Design, Measure, Analyze and Implement. The final letter stands for Control. During the Control stage, action items and schedules are implemented to ensure project outcomes are implemented. This also includes designating a person to own each action item. So, there is clear guidance on what is to be done, who is to do it, and when the action is to be complete.[2]

KING SOLOMON

When Solomon became king, he asked God to grant him wisdom. Throughout the story of him building the temple, we see he teamed with other kings and by segmenting his workers in an efficient manner to ensure the project was completed. It took eleven years for King Solomon to complete the temple. One could imagine how both physically and mentally consuming this project was for King Solomon. So, what happened when God's temple and the royal palace were completed? What does King Solomon do with his time now?

Following the temple's completion, King Solomon placed items in the temple such as the Ark of the Covenant, and other items pleasing to God. King Solomon remained faithful to God by presenting burnt offerings and taking care of what was built. Over time King Solomon amasses much wealth through others who brought him treasures so he could share his wisdom with them. After accumulating great wealth, King Solomon began to stray away from God by having relationships with women of other cultures. This went on for a long time. As he grew older King Solomon started worshiping other gods as a consequence of the influence of having many wives. When God found out about this, He cursed King Solomon and for his disobedience He warned King Solomon of the misfortune to come.[3]

King Solomon was a counsel for people both foreign and domestic. He was a gifted administrator, negotiator, and planner. Yet for all his wisdom his own desired and distraction caused him to stray from God and lose focus. When hearing about how people flocked to see and hear King Solomon's wisdom, it was probably easy for him to become complacent and think, after all he had done, he could now sit back and reap what he sowed. But, as we see what happens in the end, the desire of God was for King Solomon to remain focused and not take the talents given him for granted.[3]

Office Kaizen is another lean strategy a person can incorporate to remain focused. SLIM-IT is an acronym Office Kaizen uses to outline how to systematically organize and address problems in processes, primarily to aid with process waste elimination and standard work tasks to confirm changes are maintained. The SLIM-IT acronym stands for: Structure, Lean daily management system, Mentoring, Metrics, and while only one T is included in the acronym, it stands for: Tools, Teamwork, Training, and Technology. When beginning to incorporate SLIM-IT, an Executive Steering Team implements a Lean Daily Management Systems (LDMS). The LDMS provides focus, structure, discipline and ownership in each work group. This provides a standard method for meetings and activities to be completed. LDMS hinges on the incorporation of teamwork and technology so the SLIM-IT method is properly maintained.[4]

One final improvement strategy one can use to remain focused following project completion is utilizing the ERNIE process improvement model. This acronym stands for: Evaluate, Rank, Navigate, Implement, and Evaluate. Its foundation is based on turning the normal bell curve a project usually follows into an "S" curve. A bell curve starts close to a horizontal line, then rises as project activity increases, and then goes back close to the horizontal line as final activities are completed and a project gets into maintenance (sustain) mode. The "S" curve takes the bell and turns half of it on its side to shape an "S". The main theory behind the "S" centers on, when the project has been completed, i.e. all identified project action items have been implemented and a maintenance plan has been put in place. There is another aspect of re-evaluating the project at the new starting point to implement true continuous improvement. This is where the second Evaluate comes in. Through the incorporation of a second Evaluate, the improvement model forces users to spend time determining what the end looks like for the first project. Furthermore, establishes when the next project should be implemented to maintain a continuous improvement process.[5]

Through the periodic reinforcement of foundational principles, we are better prepared to respond when the mind starts to drift away from the main objective. A real example of this delusion in the corporate world was when ENRON, a gas and oil company, took chances with investors' money and the key company leaders deceived not only investors but their employees. Utilizing special purpose entities, ENRON executives were able to keep shady business dealings secret from investors and employees. Because of misrepresentation of financial facts, ENRON's financial position was skewed (overstated) showing positive. This fraud brought more investors to invest in ENRON. This misrepresentation of financial facts allowed key executives opportunities to embezzle the company's money and send it into bankruptcy. With the aid of the accounting firm Arthur Anderson, ENRON was able to continue to perpetrate this scheme for a brief period of time. When news of what the company was doing began to spread, the fallout was significant.[6]

Some of the sad outcomes to ENRON's failure include:

- The company went into bankruptcy,

- Thousands of employees lost their jobs, and personal savings
- New laws were enacted to aid in preventing this type of underhanded reporting from occurring in the future.[4]

While the stories of King David, King Solomon and Enron take place during different times, the main lesson learned is the fact that it is a slippery slope when we lose focus on what is important. As one traverses through life, there are many stages one goes through. With each stage comes with it new challenges and opportunities to grow. By sticking to foundational principles taught multiple times in the Bible, a person is able to remain focused. If for some reason they start to stray away, they can pull themselves back on the right path. Whether working on daily tasks, or completing a large project, focusing on the foundation will aid in remaining focused. Remembering the perspective of continuing to build off previous gains, instead of saying "it is done", aids with remaining focused on what is important.

Chapter Reflection:

1. Discuss a time when you started a project and upon completion, the desire to maintain it went away.
2. Have there been projects or improvement activities that were not maintained and the project had to be redone?
    a. Were the steps completed to do over improvements the same as were completed the last time?
    b. Was there any additional effort placed to

implement a plan to maintain improvements following completion?
3. King David spent a lot of time conquering lands and building his empire. What could he have done to stay focused on maintaining his kingdom?
4. After putting all the effort King Solomon put into building God's temple, what measures do you think he should have employed to maintain it?

CONCLUSION

Romans 8:25 NIV
But if we hope for what we do not see,
we wait for it with patience.

While this book is coming to a close, there is one final thought to consider while reading this chapter. The answer to the below question will be provided later in this chapter:

Scenario: There are five frogs sitting on a log.
Question: If four decide to jump off the log, how many are left?

The Bible contains many stories about perseverance and triumph through faith. The ones mentioned in this book are just the tip of the iceberg. During biblical days, when God's people focused on Him, big things were accomplished. Since the beginning of time, a common theme that remains important today is how each person's journey started with faith. Each person had faith that God would provide what is needed to be successful. Each person had faith that God was and is walking with them through their journey. As we close our journey, let us reflect on our Biblical examples discussed.

Beginning with God bringing everything into existence. God was deliberate in how He implemented each stage. Starting with the foundational items, God systematically moved through creation until everything was the way He wanted it. Through comparing when He created each foundational step toward initiating earth, and what He placed in His Creation, God showed how important it is to ensure time is spent working on the details. Having an end in mind, aided God by conforming what He started with would endure over time. God also understood that when He was done bringing everything into existence the statement was; "It is good" not "It is finished." It's important to remember that when a project is complete, there needs to be a plan to ensure what was accomplished is maintained.

Noah was a man who followed God through faith. He listened to God and followed the plans laid out to complete the Ark. Having a focus on ensuring that the correct resources were assembled, Noah completed the Ark and filled it with all items God had identified. Once the flood began, Noah depended on his craftmanship and God's guidance to weather the storm. Being focused on the details, Noah successfully completed his journey and delivered all creatures God had identified to weather the storm.

Moses was a man who self-imposed exile after killing a guard. He was a man who followed God's request and led the Israelites out of Egypt. Even when the Pharaoh took needed resources away and made work really hard for the Israelites, Moses remained committed to his mission. After the Pharaoh took straw away and made the guards exercise rigid discipline, God had a plan to change Pharaoh's mind. Through God's plan, Moses continued to keep the Israelites motivated even when times were rough.

David was a man of God and went on the battlefield to accomplish what God instructed him to do. Through faith, David stared down the giant and took him out with one stone. It is wise to remember the Bible verse, "One who puts on his armor should not boast like one who takes it off."[1] David's reign went through many ups and downs, but during his life he became the father of Solomon. Solomon was also a man of God. When he became king, he asked God for wisdom. Through his wisdom, Solomon's kingdom would complete building God's Temple. The main point from this is, Solomon did not try to do everything alone, but asked for help. The King of Tyre helped by providing the needed resource Solomon did not have. Hiram Abif provided the architectural skill in the building of the Temple and the direction of the laborers.

King Hezekiah was a man of God who took God's temple from being rundown, to reopening the doors of the Temple that had been closed by his father, King Ahez. By starting with the basics, King Hezekiah worked with the Levite's, opening the temple, cleaning it and re-storing practices established by King David. Utilizing available resources, when completed, God's Temple again became the location for others to come, worship and spread religious practices throughout the kingdom.

When working with fishing nets, the fishermen were focused on bringing in the largest amount of fish the nets could hold. Moving from producing a large number of products to incorporating customization in to the process. There are many alternatives for developing an efficient, process that not only provides for low cost per unit production, but also improves the customer experience through improved customer communications.

When Jesus died for our sins, the path to God was straightened. This was the ultimate improvement event in history, because prior to Jesus, the only way to be with God was by following the Ten Commandments. This has proven to be impossible for anyone except Jesus. God realized this, so the ultimate sacrifice was given. The Bible is one long story, with messages intertwined throughout. At different points throughout the Old Testament were prophesies of Jesus' coming and what would happen when he arrived.

After four hundred years of silence, Jesus was sent to teach the world about who God was. Through his actions, Jesus provided direction on how one should lead and live a life of faith. After His miraculous birth, Jesus did not begin his ministry until he was thirty years old. Prior to beginning his ministry, not a lot is said about what Jesus accomplished. From the time of his birth to when Jesus began his ministry, the only mention of him was when he was twelve years old. Jesus and his family had gone to Jerusalem for the Festival of the Passover. Following the festival, while his parents thought Jesus was with them as they travel back home, Jesus had stayed behind at the temple courts. While in the temple courts Jesus spent time listening to the teachers and asking questions. All there were amazed at his understanding and answers. When his parents found him, they had been searching Jerusalem for three days. When found, Jesus asked why they were searching, and said to them, "Didn't you know I had to be in my Father's house?"[2] More can be found in Luke 2:41-52.

Then came the crucifixion and resurrection. Through

this act, Jesus took away the requirement of following the law. When he died on the cross the curtain in the temple was torn in two, signifying a direct path to God had been established. No longer were followers bound by the Law (Ten Commandments). During his ministry, Jesus delivered messages focused on how one can develop a relationship with God.

Matthew 11:28-30, NIV

> "Come to me, all you who are weary and burdened, and I will give you rest. Take my yoke upon you and learn from me, for I am gentle and humble in heart, and you will find rest for your souls. For my yoke is easy and my burden is light."[3]

Throughout the Bible, there are many examples of regular people accomplishing big things. You are invited to dig into the Bible and find your own stories that speak to only you. Through faith, we are all called to believe God has our interests at heart, no matter the situation. The first thing we have to do is trust Him. There are going to be challenges and situations requiring one to stretch their abilities and emotional limits. Jesus focused his teachings on looking past this world through maintaining a long-term vision toward his Father. He provided a vision for believers.

Thinking back to when I was a child, the positive impact others had on me remains a big part and motivation to taking steps in learning more about God and what Jesus has done for me. When John wrote this Bible verse, Revelations 3:20, he was writing a letter to the church of Laodicea. In his letter, John told this church they were neither hot nor cold in their faith. He even went on to say he wished they were one or the other so he could properly address them. John continued by explaining his observations regarding the church's worldly behaviors. Just like this church, it takes honesty and commitment to remain dedicated to Christ's teachings.

I close with the vision that helped inspire this book. Sunday, November 10, 1985 Dr. Harrington delivered a sermon titled "The Great Invitation." During his sermon, Dr. Harrington focused on Revelations 3:20-22. After reading the verses to the congregation, he began by depicting Jesus Christ standing at a door knocking. When we give our hearts to God, everything else is His as well. Dr. Harrington continued by explaining reasons one chooses to open the door are varied widely. Some instances that might lead to doors being opened include:

- A significant personal event (death of a loved one, a person being seriously injured, etc...)
- A conversation with a friend
- A conversation with a stranger
- An event that impacts a large number of people

Reflecting on how Dr. Harrington completed his sermon each week. It is clear he was not focusing on closing the ceremony for that particular Sunday. Dr. Harrington was focused on inviting attendees by saying the act of opening the door was not the conclusion, but it was just the beginning.[4]

Now, the answer to the question posed at the beginning of this chapter. If there are five frogs sitting on a log and four decide to jump off, how many frogs are left? The number of frogs left on the log are five. Deciding to do something does not always imply that action is taken as a result of a decision. Each person discussed in this book had to make a decision and, once made, act upon it. In relation to the below Bible verse, we can decide we are going to open the door or never take action to open it to discover what is waiting for us. **You** are the only person who can open the closed door.

REVELATIONS 3:20 NIV (THE GREAT INVITATION)

"Behold, I stand at the door and knock. If anyone hears My voice and opens the door, I will come in to him and dine with him, and he with Me."[5]

Chapter Reflection:

1. At the end of the sixth day of Creation God said, "It is good." The last words Jesus said when he died on the cross were "It is finished." Discuss whether connections or what implications can be made between these two statements?
2. How will you use the information in this book to shine your light?
3. Which part of this book spoke to you the most?
4. How can the Great Invitation impact your daily life?
5. We all have had hard times and disappointments. How tough do you think it will be to respond to Jesus Christ's Great Invitation?

BENEDICTION

Go now in peace.
Remember that by the goodness of God you were born.
Remember that in the mercy of Jesus Christ you have been redeemed.
Remember that He walks beside you every day,
to comfort to strengthen and to guide: He promised he would; "Lo, I am with you always."
Remember that though others have called you servants,
He has named you friend,
In the strength of that mighty friendship,
Go forth now to serve in the Master's name,
till we meet again.
AMEN.[6]

- Dr. W. Frank Harrington

ACKNOWLEDGEMENT

This book took a good amount of time and dedication to complete. I am thankful my wife Stephanie provided me the time and understanding when my research and writing interfered with family activities. While I worked to minimize this, there were times conflicts arose. This book would not have been completed without her support. I am also thankful to have family and a group of people who spent their personal time reviewing the final draft and provide input. Those who provided a review and feedback are listed below. Their feedback helped in more ways than I can count. Thank you!!

Dr. Curtis Booher
Mr. Mark Dotson, CSSBB
Mr. Dwight Ferguson
Mrs. Beverly Ferguson
Rev. Vicki Harrington Franch
Mr. Travis Giese
Mr. Reese Harman
Mr. John Poole
Mrs. Peggy Poole
Mr. Jack Pritchard, CMBB

REFERENCES

THE BEGINNING
1. McFadden, Christopher (5/22/2017). 25 Extremely Embarrassing Architectural Failures. Retrieved from: https://interestingengineering.com/25-extremely-embarrassing-architectural-failures
2. Genesis 1:1 - 2:3, NIV
3. Douglas, Stacey (Unknown). The Project Plan; How Much Detail is Enough? Project Times. Retrieved from: https://www.projecttimes.com/articles/the-project-plan-how-much-detail-is-enough.html
4. Matthew 7:26-27, NIV
5. Halley, Henry, H. (2000). Halley's Bible Handbook. Halley's Bible Handbook Inc.

NOAH AND THE ARK
1. 2 Peter 2:5, NIV
2. Kubiak, T. M. & Benbow, Donald W. (2009). The Certified Six Sigma Black Belt Handbook. American Society for Quality. (p. 64). Second Edition. Pearson Education, Inc.

3. Fairchild, Mary. (8/5/2018). Meet Noah: A Righteous Man. Learn Religions. Retrieved from: https://www.learnreligions.com/noah-righteous-man-701200
4. Genesis 5:29, NIV
5. Unknown (2/2/2013). Project Management and Customer Requirements. Project Manage.com. Retrieved from: https://projectmanage.com/project-management-and-customer-requirements/
6. Shenkman, Dov, Johnson, Chris, and Elliott, Jason. (7/5/2016). How they Did it: Walgreens Talent Strategy. Supply Chain Management Review. Retrieved from: Retrieved from: https://www.scmr.com/article/how_they_did_it_walgreens_talent_strategy
7. Porter, Michael E. (1985). Competitive Advantage Creating and Sustaining Superior Performance. The Free Press. V. 1.
8. Halley, Henry, H. (2000). Halley's Bible Handbook. Halley's Bible Handbook Inc.
9. Ancient Code (Unknown). Ancient Sumerian accounts of the Great Flood: 'Gods' left Earth to be safe in the heavens. Ancient Code. Retrieved from: https://www.ancient-code.com/ancient-sumerian-accounts-great-flood-gods-left-earth-safe-heavens/

BRICKS WITHOUT STRAW

1. Exodus 1:1 to 2:15, NIV

2. Exodus 2:21 to 4:17, NIV
3. Exodus 5:1 through 5:21, NIV
4. Kotter, John P. (1996). Leading Change. Harvard Business School Press. p. 35-36.
5. Whitehurst, Jim. (10/13/2016). Leaders Can Shape Company Culture Through Their Behaviors. Harvard Business Review.
Retrieved from: https://hbr.org/2016/10/leaders-can-shape-company-culture-through-their-behaviors
6. Kotter, John P. (1996). Leading Change. Harvard Business School Press. p. 131-144
7. Redford, Donald B. (2001). The Oxford Encyclopedia of Ancient Egypt. Oxford University Press. Volume 1. pg. 199.
8. Daniels, Aubrey. (6/1/2016). Bringing Out the Best in People. McGraw-Hill Education. Third Edition.

DAVID AND GOLIATH
1. 1 Samuel 15-16, NIV
2. 1 Samuel 17, NIV
3. Duffy, Jill E. (5/21/2018). Bridging Research and Practice on Personal Productivity. Productivity report.
Retrieved from: https://productivityreport.org/2018/05/21/too-many-tools-problem/
4. Weitzel, Alex. (Unknown). The Importance of Providing the Right Tools at Work. Teambay.
Retrieved from: https://teambay.com/tools-at-work/

SOLOMON'S TEMPLE
1. Basu, Christian. (1/25/2019). What Core Competencies Give an Organization Competitive Advantage? Hearst Newspapers LLC.
Retrieved from: https://smallbusiness.chron.com/core-competencies-give-organization-competitive-advantage-34568.html
2. 1 Kings 5 through 6, NIV
3. Staff Report. (12/17/2013). The Right Duration for a Job Rotation. Workforce.com.
Retrieved from: https://www.workforce.com/2013/12/17/the-right-duration-for-a-job-rotation/
4. Unknown (2019). Workforce Segmentation: A Skills Based Approach. Business Performance Pty. Ltd.
Retrieved from: http://www.businessperform.com/talent-management/skills-based-workforce-segmentation.html
5. 1 Kings 6:7, NIV

CLEANING THE TEMPLE
1. 2 Chronicle 29, NIV
2. Myerson, Paul. (2012). Lean Supply Chain and Logistics Management. McGraw-Hill. p. 44-55
3. 2 Chronicles 28, NIV
4. Numbers 1:50, NIV
5. 2 Chronicles 31, NIV

REACHING THE MASSES
1. Matthew 4:19, NIV

2. Campbell, James P. (Unknown). Biblical Fishing 101 Reeling in the First Fishers of Faith, Loyola Press. Retrieved from: https://www.loyolapress.com/our-catholic-faith/prayer/arts-and-faith/culinary-arts/biblical-fishing-101-reeling-in-the-first-fishers-of-faith
3. Pettinger, Tejvan. (10/29/2009). Biography of Henry Ford. Oxford. Retrieved from: https://www.biographyonline.net/business/henry-ford.html
4. Unknown. (Unknown). Concept of Mass Production and its Advantages and Disadvantages. Retrieved from: https://businesszeal.com/mass-production
5. Kubiak, T.M.; Benbow, Donald W. (2009). The Certified Six Sigma Black Belt Handbook. Second Edition. Pearson Education. pg. 340.
6. Liker, Jeffrey. (2004). The Toyota Way 14 Management Principles from the World's Greatest Manufacturer. McGraw-Hill. pg. 130.
7. St. Augustine translated by William Findlay. From Nicene and Post Nicene fathers, First Series. (3/27/2019). St. Augustine's Commentary on the Sermon on the Mount. Crisis Magazine. Retrieved from: http://www.newadvent.org/fathers/16011.htm
8. Matthew 5, NIV
9. Westcott, Russell. (2014). The Certified Manager of Quality/Organizational Excellence Handook. Quality Press. Fourth Edition. pg. 442-443.
10. Liker, Jeffrey. (2004). The Toyota Way 14 Management

Principles from the World's Greatest Manufacturer. McGraw-Hill. pg.19-22.
11. Myerson, Paul. (2012). Lean Supply Chain and Logistics Management. McGraw-Hill. pg. 13-14.
12. Retrieved from: http://harmanice.com
13. John 2: 6-12, NIV

STAYING FOCUSED

1. 2 Samuel 10-11, NIV
2. Kubiak, T.M.; Benbow, Donald W. (2009). The Certified Six Sigma Black Belt Handbook. Pearson Education. Second Edition. pg. 403-412
3. 1 Kings 8, NIV
4. Lareau, William. (2003). Office Kaizen – Transforming Office Operations Into A Strategic Competitive Advantage. ASQ. pg. 17, 73-75.
5. Poole, Jay, (10/1/2019). Process Improvement at the North Pole with ERNIE the elf. Amazon.com. Retrieved from: https://www.amazon.com/Process-Improvement-North-Pole-ERNIE/dp/1729378714/ref=sr_1_3?keywords=jay+poole&qid=1568226545&s=gateway&sr=8-3
6. Segal, Troy. (5/29/2019). ENRON Scandal: The fall of a Wall Street Darling. Investopedia. Retrieved from: https://www.investopedia.com/updates/Enron-scandal-summary/

CONCLUSION
1. 1 Kings 20:11, NIV
2. Luke 2: 41-52, NIV
3. Matthew 28: 18-20, NIV
4. Harrington, W. Frank. (11/10/1985). The Great Invitation. Columbia Theological Seminary. W. Frank Harrington Online Sermon Collection.
   Retrieved from:
   https://www.ctsnet.edu/wp-content/themes/bd/harrington/harrington-collection-audios.php
5. Revelation 3:20, NIV
6. Benediction provided by Rev. Vicki Harrington Franch

www.ingramcontent.com/pod-product-compliance
Lightning Source LLC
Chambersburg PA
CBHW071321040426
42444CB00009B/2058